D0535680

# Shining a Penny

Published in the United States of America by Cherry Lake Publishing
Ann Arbor, Michigan
www.cherrylakepublishing.com

Reading Adviser: Marla Conn MS, Ed., Literacy specialist, Read-Ability, Inc.
Book Design: Jennifer Wahi
Illustrator: Jeff Bane

CIP data has been filed and is available at catalog.loc.gov

Printed in the United States of America
Corporate Graphics Inc.

**About the illustrator:** Jeff Bane and his two business partners own a studio along the American River in Folsom, California, home of the 1849 Gold Rush. When Jeff's not sketching or illustrating for clients, he's either swimming or kayaking in the river to relax.

# Science Notes

*Shining a Penny* explores chemical reactions. In this experiment, old pennies are dipped in three different solutions and compared. The copper oxide on old pennies dissolves best in an acidic mixture of salt and vinegar, resulting in a shiny penny.

Look at all these pennies!

They are all the same.
But they look different.

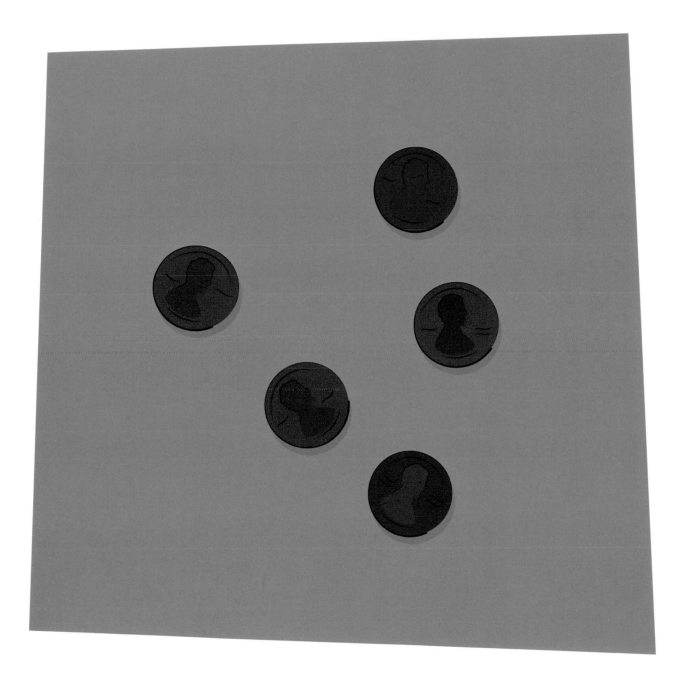

5

Some are shiny. Others are dull. Pennies get old.

They change color.

Can we find a way to clean the pennies? Can we make them shiny again?

# Let's find out!

- 3 paper cups
- Water
- Dish soap
- Vinegar
- Salt
- 15 old pennies
- Paper towels

# You will need
# these things

Line up the paper cups.

Fill the cups like this:

Cup 1: water, 5 pennies

Cup 2: water, a few drops of dish soap, 5 pennies

Cup 3: ½ cup **vinegar**, 2 teaspoons of salt (stir until the salt dissolves), 5 pennies

Leave the pennies in the cups for 5 minutes.

Remove the pennies from the cups. Put them on the paper towels. **Compare** the pennies.

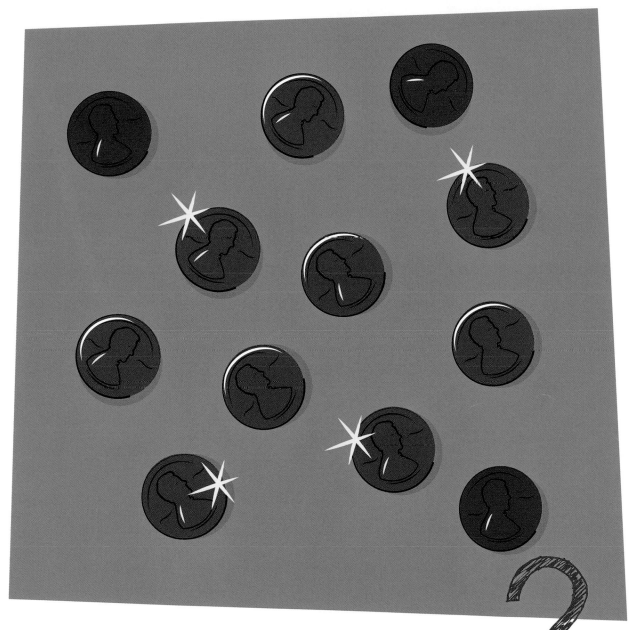

Which pennies looks the shiniest?

The vinegar pennies are clean and bright. This method works best.

Repeat the **experiment** with different liquids. Try using lemon juice, ketchup, or soda. Compare the results.

# Try different liquids!

Good job. You're done!
Science is fun!

What new questions do you have?

## glossary

**compare** (kum-PAIR) to see what is alike or different about two or more things

**experiment** (ik-SPER-uh-ment) a scientific test performed in order to learn something

**vinegar** (VIN-eh-gur) a sour liquid used in cooking and cleaning

## index